WALKING WITH THE ALMIGHTY GOD

ISAAC F. AKINDIPE

COPYRIGHT © 2020- ISAAC F. AKINDIPE
WALKING WITH THE ALMIGHTY GOD
All Rights Reserved

Scriptures marked KJV are taken from the KING JAMES VERSION (KJV): KING JAMES VERSION, public domain.

Scripture quotations marked MSG are taken from THE MESSAGE, copyright © 1993, 2002, 2018 by Eugene H. Peterson. Used by permission of NavPress. All rights reserved. Represented by Tyndale House Publishers, a Division of Tyndale House Ministries.

Scripture quotations marked (AMP) are taken from the Amplified Bible, Copyright © 1954, 1958, 1962, 1964, 1965, 1987 by The Lockman Foundation. Used by permission.

Scripture quotations marked (NIV) are taken from the Holy Bible, New International Version®, NIV®. Copyright © 1973, 1978, 1984, 2011 by Biblica, Inc.TM Used by permission of Zondervan. All rights reserved worldwide. www.zondervan.com The "NIV" and "New International Version" are trademarks registered in the United States Patent and Trademark Office by Biblica, Inc.TM

This book may not be reproduced, transmitted or stored in whole or in part by any means, including graphic, electronic or mechanical without the express written consent of the publisher except in case of brief quotations embodied in critical articles and reviews. For permission requests, write to the publisher addressed, "Attention: Permission Coordinator" at the email address below:

ifakindipe@gmail.com

ISBN: 978-1-7329979-6-7

TABLE OF CONTENTS

Introduction 1

CHAPTER ONE: The Finished Work 5

CHAPTER TWO: Dealing With The Flesh 25

CHAPTER THREE: The Journey 42

CHAPTER FOUR: Who Is God? 55

CHAPTER FIVE: Kingdom Citizens 69

Reference 90

INTRODUCTION

Walking with God is keeping and honoring a date with destiny. It is honoring our allegiance to serve in holiness, righteousness, and faithfulness all the days of our lives through Christ Jesus. It is a license and liberty given by a new birth in Christ Jesus. Walking with our Creator is like a flowing stream or river, even a sea in tandem with the dictates and directions of the tide and waves each moment. This means we allow the Potter to take the lead, and we follow suit.

Walking with God is also said to be a journey in the light. In God's presence and stride, we can neither stray nor lose focus. The flowing of the river as dictated by the waves of heaven cannot be hindered but remain steady and unstoppable. So is the man who lives by the leading and dictates of God Almighty.

Journeying with the God of Creation is a metaphoric expression that "You have arrived," "Victory at last." It's the assurance of a smooth ride to eternity and the seal of our fulfillment. It is a relationship of no looking back. It is about "Remember not the former things." New and better things are in the offing for whosoever summons up the courage to journey with God.

We cannot effectively walk with God if we have not first gotten the revelation of our seated position in Christ Jesus. Many Christians have become wary or given up in the course of their walk with God because they lack the revelation of the finished work of Christ Jesus. Hence, they journey with their strength and basic theological understanding of Scripture.

We ought not to depend on our strength but upon Jesus. Many of us today speak a spiritual language, quote scriptures, and adopt the spiritual attitudes, but everything is done with our own strength.

The Christian life does not begin with work but with rest. The Sabbath, which is the day God rested, was the first day of man. Therefore, man did not begin his journey by working but by resting. God worked for six days and rested on the seventh day, while man rested first before working. So man must first enter into God's rest before he can work. This rest is the seated position Paul was illustrating to us in his letter to the Ephesians, "And he raised us up together with Him and made us sit down together [giving us joint seating with Him] in heavenly sphere [by virtue of our being] in Christ Jesus (the Messiah, the Anointed One)" (Ephesians 2:6, Amplified Bible).

People want to serve God, obey Him, live holy, and work for Him without first sitting in Him. When you sit on a chair, it bears all of your weight, and your body is at rest. Paul shows us that we need to start our journey in Christ by sitting, not by walking. In Ephesians 1:3-14, Paul expounds the things God has done for us. He has made us His children through Jesus Christ.

Sitting begins with our new life, which has been made available to us by Jesus. That is why Paul prayed that the eyes of our understanding be enlightened (flooded with light), so we can grasp the reality of what God has done for us and where we are positioned with Jesus in heavenly places. It's just like a man in a plane. If the plane ascends the man ascends. He does not need to exert energy to ascend. Within the context of the law of gravity, he lacks the legal ground to ascend to such height on his own. However, by virtue of the fact that he is in the plane, any privileges the plane enjoys, he also enjoys.

This book will reveal to you how to walk effectively with God. It was recorded in the scriptures that mortals walked with God so much that if there was a hall of fame in heaven, they would be boldly displayed on its corridors.

Our journey must be through the finished work of Jesus Christ as we unveil how we are strategically positioned in Him in heaven. This position allows us to walk with God on the earth. When a man is in alignment with God, humanity looks at him to catch a glimpse of divinity.

CHAPTER ONE
THE FINISHED WORK

> The twenty-four elders fall down before him who sits on the throne and worship him who lives forever and ever. They lay their crowns before the throne and say: "You are worthy, our Lord and God, to receive glory and honor and power, for you created all things, and by your will they were created and have their being. (Revelation 4:10-11 NIV)

No doubt that before any other reason is given for the creation of man, we can deduce from the above passage that he was created for the good pleasure of God. He was meant to be in alignment with God, fellowship, walk, and commune with Him. His entire life was supposed to synchronize with the civilization of heaven, and by such, bring the dimensions and perspectives of the kingdom of God to the earth.

The Enemy dreaded this union, knowing full well that a man

in alignment with God is simply divinity at work upon the face of the earth. He understood that with this union, the government and economy of heaven will gain expression upon the face of the earth. As a result, he sought to colonize man to bring him under his government and economy.

God instructed man to eat of every fruit in the garden except the tree of the knowledge of good and evil. He warned that the very day he eats it, he will surely die (Genesis 2:16-17, KJV). The instruction was given to man not to eat. At that time, the woman was not present. When the man, Adam, passed the information to Eve, he added "don't touch" or you will die. In disobedience, the woman, Eve, did touch but nothing happened. Given that, she went ahead and ate the fruit.

Everyone who preaches or teaches the Word of God must learn to give the accurate interpretation. We must be careful not to add what God did not say or remove what God said. If we do so, we will be stumbling blocks hindering people from walking with God effectively.

The Enemy's target was the man. He used the woman to get to the man because the man was the carrier of the seed. Eve was the one who was deceived; however, Adam knew exactly what he was doing. He placed his love for his wife above his obedience to God. That is why Jesus said to walk with Me, you will have to hate your father, mother, wife, children, brothers, and sisters (Luke 14:26, KJV).

Adam was still in the garden; yet, God was looking for him: "Adam, where are you?" Likewise, many people are in the church today, but they are not in God. They are working for God but not walking with Him. The Enemy thought he had succeeded in his plan and man was doomed. But God interrupted his celebration with good news. The womb of a woman was being designed in such a way that she would not need sexual intercourse with a man to get pregnant; all she needed was a seed. That is why God said, "I will put enmity between you and the woman, between your seed and her seed, it will bruise your head and you will bruise his heel" (Genesis 3:15). God only made reference to the seed of the woman, not that of the man. That seed was Jesus.

The Enemy, in a bid to ensure men do not align with God to bring to pass His will and purpose upon the earth has always caused men to rebel against God.

The story of Cain and Abel represents two classes: the righteous and the wicked, the believers and the unbelievers. Abel was a man who walked with God. He was in alignment with God. He did not go to a Bible school to understand that a blood sacrifice was required. In fact, under the law, almost everything is purified by means of blood. Without the shedding of blood, there is neither release from sin and its guilt nor the remission of the due and merited punishment of sins (Hebrew 9:22, KJV).

Cain was not walking with God. He presented an unacceptable sacrifice. He murdered Abel out of envy and is a representation of the wicked who are envious of the righteous. He is a depiction of the wicked who persecute the righteous because their right living, alignment, and walk with God condemn them of their sinful nature.

THE BLESSED MAN

The journey of man did not begin with work but with rest. We earlier established that after God created everything, the first day of man was the day He rested. God and man had fellowship with each other. However, the fall of man broke that fellowship. Man walked in the counsel of the wicked. Psalm Chapter 1 describes what that looks like.

> Blessed (happy, fortunate, prosperous, and enviable is the man who *walks* and lives not in the counsel of the ungodly [following their advice, their plans and

purpose], nor ***stands*** [submissive and inactive], in the path where sinners walk, nor ***sits*** down [to relax and rest] where the scornful [and the mockers] gather, (2) But his delight and desire are in the law of the Lord, and on His law (the precepts, the instructions, the teachings of God) he habitually meditates (ponders and studies) by day and by night. (3) And he shall be like a tree firmly planted [and tended] by streams of water, ready to bring forth its fruits in its season; it's leaf also shall not fade or wither; and everything he does shall prosper [and come to maturity]. (Psalm 1:1-3, AMP)

Jesus came to restore man back to his original place in God. Man's journey, as it did in the beginning, starts with the finished work of Christ. Jesus declared on the cross, "It is finished."

Paul's letter to the Ephesians can be divided into three parts. The first portrays the position of the believer in Christ: "And He raised us up together with Him and made us sit down together [giving us joint seating with Him] in heavenly sphere [by virtue of our being] in Christ Jesus (the Messiah, the Anointed One)" (Ephesians 2:6, AMP).

The second part illustrates our walk with God that reflects in how we live in the world: "I therefore the prisoner for the

Lord, appeal to and beg you to walk (lead a life) worthy of the [divine] calling to which you have been called [with behavior that is credit to the summons to God's service" (Ephesians 4:1).

The third part reveals to us how we must handle the Enemy: "Put on God's whole armor [the armor of a heavy-armed soldier which God supplies], that you may be able successfully to stand up against [all] the strategies and deceits of the devil" (Ephesians 6:11, KJV).

In this book of Ephesians, Paul shows us that the life of a believer consists of sitting with Christ, walking by Him and standing in Him. Our emphasis in this book, however, is on our walk with God. But we can never fully understand how to walk with God if we don't first know how to sit in Christ.

THE LIFE IS IN THE BLOOD

All men are related by blood, by the blood of Adam, which is sinful and polluted, dead in trespasses and sin. All men have a common origin from Adam. Adam's blood flows through the veins of every human being whether black or white, Jew or Gentile. This blood carries a sentence of death because of Adam's sin. For this reason, all men die a common death with no exceptions.

Remember the life is in the blood: "For the life (the animal soul) is in the blood, and I have given it for you upon the altar to make atonement for your souls; for it is the blood that makes atonement, by reason of the life [which it represents]" (Leviticus 17:11, KJV).

When man ate of the fruit of the knowledge of good and evil, it resulted in death. His blood was poisoned. Therefore, everyone related to Adam by birth still succumb to that poison of sin, which is transmitted through the blood.

Man was formed from the dust, lifeless, "And God breathed into his nostrils the breath of life, and man became a living soul" (Genesis 2;7B, KJV). The breath of life brought about the blood. Life is in the blood. Adam's body was of the ground but his blood was a separate gift of God.

When man ate of the tree of knowledge of good and evil, he died spiritually, which gradually progressed to physical death. The blood of man became polluted by sin. Sin is not in the body but in the blood. The body becomes sinful because it's nourished by the blood.

The very fact that sin is in the blood necessitated the virgin birth of Christ if He was the son of Adam, yet, without sin. Jesus could partake of Adam's flesh, which is not inherently sinful. However, He could not partake of the blood that is completely polluted with sin. God had already made a way for Jesus to be born without partaking of the sin of Adam. Jesus did not have a single drop of Adam's blood in His veins; therefore, He did not share in Adam's sin.

The very fact that sin is in the blood means the only way sin can be atoned is when sinless blood is provided by someone who is entirely sinless, someone who is not affected by the sin of Adam, yet, belongs to the human race. Something transpired in the garden after Adam and Eve had eaten of the forbidden fruit, and they saw they were naked. The first thing they did was make garments of fig leaves. They tried to proffer a solution for their error. People do the same thing today. They formulate strategies, traditions, cultures, religious concepts, and technology all in a bid to cover up the deficiency of fallen man. But it is to no avail because the only solution for sin is in God.

When God stepped on the scene, He covered Adam and Eve with coats of skin. Although blood was not directly used here, we know by implication that the coat of skin could not be obtained without the death of an innocent animal. It took the death of an animal to atone for the sin of Adam, not his futile effort to cover his error. Salvation must be of God. "If we say that we have no sin, we deceive ourselves and the truth is not in us. If we confess our sins, he is faithful to forgive us our sins, and to cleanse us from all unrighteousness" (1 John 1:8-9, KJV).

The demand of the law is for perfection or death; therefore, God in His infinite mercy also gave Moses a design for the tabernacle because He knew the Israelites could not keep the law. The central object of the tabernacle was the ark, which contained three items: the golden pot of manna, Aaron's rod, and two stone tablets on which God had written the Ten Commandments.

These items were actually symbols of man's rebellion. The golden pot of manna represents man's rejection of God's provision. The rod of Aaron represents man's rejection of God's leadership, and the two tablets of God's commandment represent man's rejection of His standard of holiness. But because God delights in mercy, He had these items put away in the ark and covered with the mercy seat, which had two cherubim on it.

Once every year, the priest would enter the Holy of Holies where the ark was and sprinkle the blood of the animal sacrifice on the mercy seat. Whenever God came down, He saw the blood on the mercy seat, not the rebellion of men. He saw the blood and accepted the people.

Today, Jesus is our High Priest. He has sprinkled His own blood on the true mercy seat in heaven.

By such means, therefore, it was necessary for the

[earthly] copies of heavenly things to be purified, but the actual heavenly things themselves [required far] better and nobler sacrifices than these, 24. For Christ (the Messiah) has not entered into a sanctuary made with hands, only a copy and pattern of the true one, but [He has entered] into heaven itself, now to appear in the [very] presence of God on our behalf. 25. Nor did He [enter into the heavenly sanctuary to] offer Himself regularly again and again, as the High priest enters the [Holy of] holies every year with blood not his own. 26. For then would He often have had to suffer [over and over again] since the foundation of the world. But as it now is, He has once and for all at the consummation and close of ages appeared to put away and abolish sin by His sacrifice of Himself. (Hebrew 9:23-26, AMP)

The blood of Jesus was sinless and perfect; therefore, it was incorruptible. Consequently, we who are in Christ have a perfect standing before God forever.

The Cross

Jesus did not only die in the place of sinners to give them eternal life and restore their relationship with God. He also took sinners with Him to the cross. Many Christians miss out on this truth. They think Jesus only died for them and don't really understand He took them to the cross also. What happened on the cross was not just a substitution but also co-death. What do I mean by this?

The effects of salvation will not be complete if it is only limited to the substitution (Jesus replacing us on the cross) because we still live in a world filled with temptations. After being saved, the believer finds himself contending with the sinful nature. He finds it difficult to overcome sin. Jesus saved sinners from the penalty of sin by dying for them on the cross. He delivered sinners from the power of sin, which is the old man, by taking them to the cross.

Since the fall of man, we have all inherited the sinful nature. Sin does not come from outside. Rather, it resides on the inside. Temptation comes from outside and whenever it does, the old man on the inside responds and sin is committed. The old man, which is the sin factor, is corrupted beyond repair. It cannot be remade. God dealt with it by putting it to death.

To satisfy the claims of divine justice against humanity, Jesus had to deal with the sin problem. Sin is a spiritual thing, so it must be dealt with in the spirit realm. All of the good and bad in Adam are concluded in the death of Christ.

"For he that is dead is freed from sin. Sin does not come from outside it is there within us, it is temptation that comes from outside, and that sin that dwells within us is the old man that is corrupted" (Romans 6:7, KJV).

"Now if I do what I do not desire to do, it is no longer I that is doing it [it is not myself that acts], but the sin [principle] which dwells within me, fixed and operating within me" (Romans 7:20, AMP).

Sinful man has the sin factor in him, so whenever outside temptation comes, it responds from within, and the result of that response is sin. According to the scriptures, our sins are cleansed by the blood. However, it was never written that the old man is cleansed by the blood. The old man must be crucified (co-death). Believers must understand they cannot crucify the old man by himself. It must be done through union with Jesus Christ.

> We know that our old (unrenewed) self was nailed to the cross with Him in order that our body which is instrument of sin might be made ineffective and inactive for evil, that we might no longer be slaves of sin. 7. For when a man dies, he is freed (loosed, delivered) from the power of sin among men. 8. Now if we have died with Christ, we believe that we shall also live with him. (Romans 6:6-8, AMP)

The purpose of having our old man crucified was to set us free from the control of sin.

"When Jesus died, he took sin down with him, but alive he brings God down to us" (Romans 6:10, Message).

"Even so consider yourselves also dead to sin and your relation to sin broken but alive to God, living in unbroken fellowship with Him in Christ Jesus" (Romans 6:11, AMP).

You don't deal with the old man by trying to feel it. You must consider it dead! Another version of the Bible says you must reckon it dead. For so long as we live in these mortal bodies, the sinful nature will co-exist with us. It cannot be annihilated. We can only deliver it to death by the power of the cross and render it powerless.

Jesus' death on the cross was long and painful. He was on the cross for a very long time. Moreover, He was even advised to save Himself and come down to prove He was truly the Son of God. Truth is He could have come down. But He chose not to. The Devil will put severe pressure on the believer who is being crucified with Jesus on the cross to come down. Therefore, you must be watchful.

When believers are negligent, the Devil's temptations will manifest. As soon as the outside temptation arrives, the old man will respond. It is therefore important to return the ground of the cross at that moment. As you reckon yourself as dead, the Holy Spirit will apply the power of the cross to you so that temptation immediately loses its attraction.

OUR POSITION IN GOD

The chief priests and Pharisee assemblies went to Pilate to inform him of what Jesus said before He died. In their words: "We have just remembered how that vagabond imposter said while He was alive, after three days I will rise again" (Matthew 27:63, AMP). They got the approval from Pilate to secure and safeguard the tomb to the best of their knowledge. So they sealed the tomb and placed soldiers to watch with their physical eyes what was going to transpire in the spirit realm.

On Sunday morning, the very soldiers were on the ground like dead men. They had witnessed something beyond human imagination. They had seen that the grave, the stone, their weapons, skills, and experience in war lacked potency against the angel that came. These men would have been in the best position to pass this message to their generation, for they witnessed it live. However, the chief priests and elders gave the soldiers sufficient money to keep their mouths shut, to subvert the truth.

Many today for the sake of something to eat and drink, refuse to pass the message God gave them to their generation. The messages have been subverted. The minstrels that have keys to tap into the music room in heaven and draw dimensions in heaven to the earth when they minister, now sing for the Enemy. Talents have been subverted for the sake of fame and what to eat and drink.

Nothing was ever recorded about these soldiers again because they worked for men and got their reward from men. They walked with men instead of God and lost relevance in eternity.

Jesus rose from the grave and ascended to heaven to present the blood once and for all in the Holy of Holies. That blood is still speaking for us today. Among the pieces of furniture described in the tabernacle, no provision was made for a chair. This signifies that the work of the priest was not complete.

> Furthermore, every human priest stands at his altar of service ministering daily, offering the same sacrifices over and over again which never are able to strip from every side of us the sins that envelop us and take them away. Whereas this one, Christ, after He had offered a single sacrifice for our sins that shall avail for all time, sat down at the right hand of God. (Hebrew 10:11-12, AMP)

In the case of our High Priest, He sat down, unlike the Old Testament priests.

That the God of our Lord Jesus Christ, the Father of glory, may give unto you the spirit of wisdom and revelation in the knowledge of him: The eyes of your understanding being enlightened; that ye may know what is the hope of His calling, and what the riches of the glory of his inheritance in the saints, And what is the exceeding greatness of his power to us-ward who believe, according to the working of his mighty power, which he wrought in Christ, when he raised him from the dead, and set him at his own right hand in heavenly places, far above principality, and power, and might, and dominion, and every name that is name that is named, not only in this world, but also in that which is to come. (Ephesians 1:17-21, KJV)

Every believer ought to pray and ask God to open their eyes to the deep realities of the finished work of Jesus. This is significant because you cannot walk in the fullness of that reality if you cannot see it. Paul revealed to us again that Jesus is not seated alone in heavenly places, but we are seated in Him.

"And raised us up with him, and made us to sit with him in heavenly places, in Christ Jesus: ... for by grace have ye been saved through faith; and that not of yourselves, it is the gift of God; not of works, that no man should glory" (Ephesians 2:6-9, AMP).

The Christian life does not begin with a walk but with sitting in Christ. To sit means to be in a position in which the upper body is upright and the legs, especially the upper legs are supported by an object. When a man is seated, the weight of his body is carried by the chair, unlike when he is walking. Many believers have subscribed to the error that they must walk before they sit.

Paul began by revealing to us how God has blessed us with spiritual blessings in Christ in heavenly places. When you walk, you exert effort. However, when you sit, you rest. Paul drew our attention to the very fact that we are saved, not by works but by grace…through faith (Ephesians 2:8, KJV).

As mentioned before, on the account of creation, God worked for six days and rested on the seventh day—the Sabbath day. The first day of man was this very day that God rested. Hence, man rested before he worked. Many believers have been wired to believe they must work hard before they can sit. In other words, they must work for their blessings and salvation. But Scripture helps us understand that while we were yet sinners, Jesus died for us because of God's love (Romans 5:8). It had nothing to do with our actions.

When the Israelites journeyed from Egypt, God tried to bring them into the place of His rest. However, they were used to hard labor in Egypt and programmed in that manner so much that regardless of the miracles God did, they still believed they needed to earn His love. God showed them their victory had nothing to do with their efforts but with His finished work. All they needed to do was believe and co-operate to bring to pass an expected end (Hebrews 3:10-11, KJV).

When the people complained for water, instead of communicating their desires to God, God instructed Moses to strike the rock with his rod. The elders stood as witnesses and saw the effects of Moses' obedience. Water came out of the rock (Exodus 17:6, KJV). In this very first act, effort was applied, which is a reflection of the belief system of the people that God cannot provide for them. They must work for everything as they did in Egypt.

Not too long after when they got to Kadesh, they grumbled again for the lack of water, but this time, God instructed Moses to take the rod in his hand and speak (Numbers 20:8, KJV). Here, God was bringing them into another dimension of their walk with Him. He was opening their eyes to the very fact that they are loved, not as a result of their actions, so they should come into a place of *koinonia* (communion with God). This is a place where they communicate with God and believe in Him, to operate from a perspective of what He has done and not what they can do.

Moses struck the rock, instead of communicating, to reveal to the people a dimension of *koinonia*. He wanted them to understand what God did, to agree and bring to pass that thing in the realm of mortals.

"Come, for all things are now ready" (Luke 14:17, KJV).

Our Christian journey begins with discovering what God has provided. The outpouring of the Holy Spirit was a function to exalt Jesus. It had nothing to do with what men did (Acts 2:33, KJV). What did you do to be born again? Nicodemus thought he needed to work his way back into his mother's womb for him to be born again (John 3:3-5, KJV). But Jesus explained to Him we only receive the born-again experience from God. When you try to do everything on your own, you place yourself back under the law. Such works are regarded as dead works.

The church today has a problem similar to what we see with the elder brother in the story of the prodigal son. The elder brother worked very hard; yet, he did not know his rights as a son. He tried so hard to please his father when his father was already pleased. On the other hand, the younger brother regardless of his errors understood his rights as a son. He returned home and was welcomed. The point is the father of these two boys did not love them because of what work they did or did not do. He loved them regardless.

Our journey begins with the finished work of God.

CHAPTER TWO

DEALING WITH THE FLESH

"For as many that are led by the spirit of God, they are the sons of God" (Romans 8:14, KJV).

Any man born of a woman is of the flesh. He is a natural man. He is naturally sinful and spiritually dead. Natural man is perverse, corrupt, and deceitful. The way of a natural man is a way of unrighteousness. It is a path of evil. It disobeys the commands and instructions of God Almighty.

A natural man threads on a broad and slippery path that terminates in eternal damnation. The heart of a natural man is full of dust. Two things that resemble are always compared. Opposite characters cannot navigate successfully. Hence, the new birth in Christ Jesus is essential to do away with the old Adamic nature.

A man whose life is embedded in the fruits of the flesh cannot walk with the Most Righteous God. Therefore, the need for a new birth or being born again is incontestable. Regeneration is borne out of the unalloyed love of God our Creator. It is of immense significance to all flesh, all who want to make it to the eternal kingdom.

FREE WILL

When God created man, He gave him free will to eat from any of the trees in the garden, except the tree of the knowledge of good and evil. God directed man what to do and told him the consequences he would face should he default. Man had a choice. Man would have been a machine if he had been created without a will. It is the organ for his decision making.

Before the fall, the will of man was in sync with the will of God. After the fall, Cain operated in the opposite direction of God's will, as he moved out of Eden, the presence of God. Cain started a different civilization. In moving out of Eden, he relocated from under God's radar where his will was subject to the will of God. Cain built a city that God was not part of its foundation. We see how much man can achieve without God, for man was created with several abilities.

God's will was for man to dominate the earth. However, as said earlier, man, operating in the flesh, always seeks to oppose the will of God. For example, the men who found a place in Shinar to build a tower that would reach into the heavens (Genesis 11:1-9, KJV). We can see several skills on display.

Man is endowed with many gifts. In exercising his will, he can live completely contrary to the pattern of God. This is a more cogent reason why man must walk daily after the Spirit. "For the flesh lusteth against the Spirit, and the Spirit against the flesh: and these are contrary the one to the other: so that ye cannot do the things that ye would" (Galatians 5:17, KJV). Man can only obey God when he is walking in the Spirit.

The salvation of man occurs when his will is brought into obedience to God by believing in the Word of God. He receives the Holy Spirit, and his will is renewed. Genuine salvation is simply being delivered from self and united with God. "This I say walk in the spirit and ye shall not fulfill the lust of the flesh" (Galatians 5:16, KJV). In walking with God, we must realize it is not about what we value or hold in high esteem but what God values.

If man had no will, he would be nothing more than a robot. However, man was created with the power to make choices. Hence, he is held responsible for his actions. "O Jerusalem, Jerusalem, thou that killest the prophets..., how often would I have gathered thy children together, even as a hen gathereth her chickens under her wings, and ye would not" (Matthew 23:37, KJV). As much as it was the will of God to bring this people close to Him, He did not force it on them. They chose not to submit to Him.

On the other hand, Jesus submitted His will to the will of the Father as we saw in Gethsemane: "He went a little farther on, threw himself face downwards on the ground, and prayed, My Father, if it is possible, take this cup of suffering from, yet not what I want but what you want" (Matthew 26:39).

Jesus had gained mastery in His walk with God. He was able to submit completely to God although He had the liberty to continue or stop. He said to Peter, "Don't you know that I could call on my Father for help, and at once He would send me more than twelve armies of angels" (Matthew 26:53).

Some people think overcoming sin is all that's necessary, but they don't know the greatest battle is against self. No enemy from outside can conquer a man who has first conquered himself.

The plan of salvation is the will of God, for man cannot save himself. "Having predestinated us unto the adoption of children by Jesus, Christ to himself, according to the good pleasure of His will" (Ephesians 1:5, KJV). That being said, man still has a role to play by accepting the gift of salvation. Though predestinated from the very beginning, he must still come to the point where he submits his will, personal ambitions, and dreams to walk with the Father. As he walks, the blueprints of his destiny are unveiled bit by bit.

Spiritual maturity has nothing to do with age as Jesus explicitly tells Peter. "I am telling you the truth when you were young you used to get ready and go anywhere you wanted to, but when you are old, you will stretch out your hands and someone else will bind you and take you where you don't want to go" (John 21:18, Good News).

Growing up, at some point, your parents held your hands and took you to places you might not have desired to go. Gradually, you grew to a stage where you sought their consent before taking certain decisions. Then you got to a certain age when you no longer sought their permission because you were deemed mature enough and responsible for your actions. Within the physical context, we call this maturity.

In the spiritual context, as illustrated by the passage above, when you were a child, not yet come into the spiritual reality, you did whatever you liked and went to the places you desired. However, when you are born into the spiritual reality, you need the Holy Ghost to hold your hand and guide you to your destination. You begin to realize that life is more spiritual. It's not a question of what you want and what you like. To successfully navigate spiritual pathways, you need the Holy Ghost.

The shape of the world is heaven first and then the earth. But the carnal man is so blind all he sees is the earth. He lives as if nothing exists outside the physical. But that's not true. With the guidance of the Holy Spirit, you will be taken to places you normally would not have gone as a carnal man. You may also be asked to do what you don't like to do.

God told Abraham to sacrifice his only son to Him. Of course, Abraham did not want to do that. He still had every power to say no to God. However, on the course of his spiritual journey, he had gained God's perspective. He no longer lived based on what he felt was right. It was no longer a question of his intelligence. Rather, He lived according to the will of the Ancient of Days.

This is the dimension of sons, "For as many as are led by the Spirit of God, they are the sons of God" (Romans 8:14, KJV). You get two job offers. Logically speaking, the one with the highest pay is preferable considering you have bills to pay. But God says go for the one with the lesser pay without a logical explanation. Your response will determine your level of growth spiritually. Your actions are no longer to bring you glory but to bring glory to God.

Circumcision

Elijah was to be taken up to heaven in a whirlwind. He was led by the Spirit of God to journey through four places with Elisha: Gilgal, Bethel, Jericho, and Jordan. Each of these places has spiritual significance. Gilgal means "rolled away."

> At that time the LORD said unto Joshua, Make thee sharp knives, and circumcise again the children of Israel the second time. 3. And Joshua made him sharp knives, and circumcised the children of Israel at the hill of the foreskins... 8. And it came to pass, when they had done circumcising all the people that they abode in their places in the camp, till they were whole. 9. And the Lord said unto Joshua, this day have I rolled away the reproach of Egypt from off you. Wherefore the name of the place is Gilgal unto this day. (Joshua 5:2-9, KJV)

The Israelites who came out of Egypt were circumcised, but those from the generation born afterward were not. Hence, they needed to get rid of the old flesh. The fact that their fathers were circumcised was not reason enough for them to be uncircumcised. In the Old Testament, circumcision was of the flesh but in the New Testament, it was a matter of the heart. "Ye stiff-necked and uncircumcised in heart and ears, ye do always resist the Holy Ghost: as your fathers did, so do ye" (Acts 7:51, KJV). The Bible says this generation was about to enter the Promised Land and there was a need for them to do away with the old flesh. It points out the fact that the flesh profits nothing. Circumcision is not a very pleasant experience. Joshua was instructed to make sharp knives for the procedure. The pain was so much, the men could not move.

Sometimes, we will have to make painful decisions in life. Circumcision deals with your flesh to the extent you can no longer depend on your strength, human intellect, and wisdom. You have to entirely depend on God.

We can trace the origin of circumcision to Abraham. God instructed him to circumcise himself, his descendants and his entire household, which was a token of covenant between him and God (Genesis 17:1-14).

God gave Abraham and his descendants the mark of circumcision as a physical reminder they were to be cut out from the world and serve only the one true God. "Circumcise yourselves to the Lord, remove the foreskin of your hearts, O men of Judah and inhabitants of Jerusalem, lest my wrath go forth like fire, and burn that none quench it, because of the evil of your doing" (Jeremiah 4:4, KJV). These people were circumcised in their skin. However, this was only a pointer to the fact that they must be circumcised in their hearts. In other words, God wanted them to have pure hearts separated unto Him.

Many people are working for God but very few are walking with Him. Many are working actively, but God requires you to walk heartily. A heart that is not circumcised is simply a heart that is disobedient to the Holy Spirit.

In Deuteronomy 10:14-16, KJV, it is illustrated to us that the entire world belongs to God: the heavens, earth, and everything in it. Yet, He chose for Himself a people from the world. Circumcision was the mark that differentiated them from everyone else. We judge by appearances. God judges by the content of the heart.

Stephen stood before the council and told them they were uncircumcised in their hearts because they always resisted the Holy Ghost. They were circumcised in the flesh but that made no difference to their inner beings. They were still stiff-necked because they depended on their human abilities. They worshipped God with their lips, but their hearts were far away.

> For we [Christians] are the true circumcision, who worship God in spirit and by the Spirit of God and exult and glory and pride ourselves in Jesus Christ, and put no confidence or dependence on what we are in the flesh

and on outward privileges and physical advantages and external appearances. (Philippians 3:3, KJV)

Paul, speaking in the preceding verse states that those who worship God in spirit and by the Spirit are the circumcision. Therefore, it is possible to be born again but still not come to this reality of circumcision where you no longer depend on the flesh but on the Holy Ghost.

"And the Lord thy God will circumcise thine heart, and the heart of thy seed, to love the Lord thy God with all thine heart, and with all thy soul, that thou mayest live" (Deuteronomy 30:6, KJV). God knows that man cannot circumcise his heart except by the Holy Ghost. "Create in me a clean heart, O God, and renew a right spirit within me. Do not cast me away from thy presence, and do not take thy Holy Spirit from me. Restore to me the joy of thy salvation, and sustain me with a willing spirit" (Psalm 51:10-12, KJV).

The Holy Spirit performs the circumcision of the heart. Deuteronomy 10:16 tells us to circumcise the foreskin of our hearts, and Deuteronomy 30:6, KJV says God will circumcise the foreskin of our hearts. For circumcision to be effective, we have a role to play by submitting to God. His role is to work on our hearts. The ordinance of circumcision was an outward physical sign of one's willingness to obey God and be one of His chosen people.

Under the new covenant, God is calling a spiritual nation composed of individuals converted and regenerated by the Holy Spirit. The people of God are now circumcised spiritually. The physical circumcision was only a pointer to what was to come, the circumcision of the heart.

"But he is a Jew, which is inwardly; and circumcision is of the heart, in the spirit, and not in the letter; whose praise is not of men but of God" (Romans 2:29, KJV).

"Forasmuch as ye are manifestly declared to be the epistle of Christ ministered by us, written not with ink, but with the Spirit of the living God; but in fleshly tables of the heart" (2 Corinthians 3:3, KJV).

The circumcision of the male child on the eighth day is symbolic. The number seven stands for perfection, and the additional day restarts the circle, a new day. The man circumcised on the eighth day is a new man because he has agreed to circumcise the foreskin of his heart.

The Grain of Wheat

> I assure you, most solemnly I tell you, unless a grain of wheat falls into the earth and dies, it remains, just one grain; it never becomes more but lives by itself alone. But if it dies, it produces many others and

yields a rich harvest. 25. Anyone who loves his life loses it, but anyone who hates his life in this world shall keep it to life eternal. Whoever has no love for, no concern for, no regard for his life here on earth, but despises it, preserves his life forever and ever. (John 12:24-25, AMP)

Jesus described life as a grain of wheat that must die. He went on to say he who loves his life in this world will lose it, and he who hates his life in this world shall keep it. Man is willing to lose everything except life. Yet, we are asked to lose our lives. This very life is our natural life; it is composed of our will, intellect, and affection. If man allows this life to be the central point, the focus, and very driving force of his entire existence on the earth then he will lose eternal life.

The outer shell of a grain of wheat is very attractive. At best, it would be admired and can be displayed for everyone to see. However, it is of no use if it remains in that state. The grain must undergo a process of death. It must lose its attractiveness and be buried. Inevitably, the soil will do great damage to its beauty.

If we want to be useful and productive, we must be prepared to die to the flesh. If that outer shell is composed of love for this mundane world, it will die. However, if your love is redirected to God, you will no longer operate or live by your intellect but by the guidance of the Holy Spirit. You will die to the flesh (Romans 8:13, KJV). Dying to the flesh is a daily activity. It is completely denying yourself from ruling you.

Many find this process difficult because it means trusting another. Life is in the grain, but it will not gain expression because the outer shell is a hindrance. The seed falling into the earth is a symbol that it has yielded itself for the earth to break its outer shell. That which it holds in high esteem will be dealt with.

For the Holy Spirit to operate through man, the outward man, which is the outer shell must be broken. In doing so, external factors are employed to break down the outer man. Just as the ground has an impact on breaking the outer shell of the grain, trials and certain external forces are employed to break the outer man.

The inward man is the spirit, and the outward man is the soul. For the Holy Spirit who resides in our inward man to gain expression through the outward man, the outward man must be broken.

"May He grant you out of the rich treasury of His glory to be strengthened and reinforced with mighty power in the inner man by the Holy Spirit Himself indwelling in your innermost being and personality" (Ephesians 3:16, KJV).

"To the degree that you yield to the Spirit of God, and the word of God will determine the degree you will be changed by God" (Theodore Dones).

"For I reckon that the sufferings of this present time are not worthy to be compared with the glory which shall be revealed in us." (Romans 8:18, KJV).

The rod in Moses' hand helped him to protect Jethro, his father-in-law's flock. That was until he encountered God in the backside of the desert. Moses seemed comfortable with his life and gave God several reasons why he could not do His bidding. For as long Moses decided to operate according to his bidding, the rod remained his and would do no more than keep the flock. However, when he decided to submit to God and the rod became the rod of God, it performed miracles. The next time he was instructing Joshua in the battle with Amalek, he said, "I will stand on the top of the hill with the rod of God in mine hand" (Exodus 17:9).

The rod of Moses became the rod of signs and wonders when he decided to obey God. It was by that rod he performed the supernatural in Egypt and led the children of Israel out of that land.

Until a grain of wheat falls to the ground and dies, it abides alone. The ground is the place of surrender where you no longer operate by emotions and intelligence but by the leading of the Spirit.

A rich young man came to Jesus and in his interaction with the Master he made it clear he had fulfilled all the requirements of the law. He was very obedient to the Ten Commandments. Nevertheless, Jesus told him to go and sell his properties and give the money to the poor. And in doing so, he would receive treasure in heaven. Jesus told Him when he was finished distributing his wealth, he should return and follow Him (Matthew 19:21-22, KJV).

You see, the thing about the death of the grain is that, in death, external factors are employed to break that outer shell so that life on the inside will gain expression. God will place demands on the things you hold in high esteem, the things you place so much hope and dependence on, the things that make the society celebrate you. He will ask you to surrender them. The rich young man became sorrowful.

Perhaps you have been working in the church for years. You have been faithful to service. Yet, you hold some things so dear to your heart they are hindering you from being fruitful. Several times, God has placed a demand on those things, but you will not let go.

Maybe you are like Peter. You might hold a first-class degree in fishery. You know the waters very well. You know the exact time the fishes will assemble at strategic locations. You have so much experience in your work you even received the award of the best fisherman in the entire town. You are well-known all over the world. Yet, in the volume of the book written concerning you, it is recorded that you were meant to be a fisher of men.

For every record set in time by the flesh, a day will come that another will rise and beat that record. Until a grain of wheat falls to the ground and dies, it will not yield fruits that are fruits indeed from which generations yet unborn will benefit.

On that day by the lake of Gennesaret (Luke 5:3-7, KJV), the Lord needed a platform to minister to the people, and He chose Peter's ship. Peter had to surrender his boat to the Lord. When Jesus had finished ministering to the people from the ship, He instructed Peter to cast his net on the right side. He seemed to be saying to Peter, "You have been operating by your intelligence for so long; now, let Me show the difference between what is good and what is right. Cast thy net to the right side."

Peter acknowledged the fact that he had been operating by his intelligence for a long time. Now, he would operate by the directive of the Word of God. The result was a net-breaking harvest. This was an indication that Peter was meant to be a fisher of men. On the Day of Pentecost, three thousand souls were added to the church after his first sermon.

Jonah could hear from God; yet, his outer man was too thick to allow God to operate through him. God instructed him to go to Nineveh and cry against the city. Instead, Jonah chose to embark on a personal voyage to Tarshish. God sent a great wind and storm that started to break the ship.

Some storms in our lives are not actually meant for destruction. They are there to break the outer man, so we will yield completely to the leading of God. The mariners threw Jonah in the sea, but God, in His omniscience and divine wisdom had prepared a great fish to swallow Jonah for three days. It was like the grain of wheat falling into the ground. Jonah came out as a new man. The entire nation of Nineveh was saved by the coming of a man who had undergone the death process. If Jonah had succeeded in running to Tarshish, his name would have been lost forever.

CHAPTER THREE

THE JOURNEY

And Terah took Abram his son, and Lot the son of Haran, his son's son, and Sarah his daughter in law, his son Abram's wife; and they went forth with them from Ur of Chaldees, to go into the land of Canaan; and they came to Haran, and there they dwelt. [32] And the days of Terah were two hundred and five years: and Terah died in Haran. (Genesis 11:31-32, KJV)

Stephen, speaking in the book of Acts 7:2-4, KJV, reveals to us how the God of glory appeared to Abraham in Mesopotamia, before the move from the Ur of Chaldees to Haran. From the above passage, we can clearly see the call was for him to go to Canaan. The journey they embarked on from Chaldees was toward Canaan, but along the way, they came across a land where they decided to settle down.

We have been called like Abraham out of the system of the world to find and fulfill our purpose in God. "For many are called but few are chosen" (Matthew 22:14, KJV). Being chosen with respect to the call is based on your decision to cooperate with God's eternal purpose in your life.

God chose us first and then called us according to His eternal purpose so that when we chose Him, we become the chosen. There was no way Abraham could fulfill his destiny in Babylon. God had to call him out to separate him for a purpose. The first thing God does is separate, so we can focus on Him. Walking with God requires focus, but there are many things in the world to distract us.

Haran was one such place that served as a distraction. Abraham stopped in Haran, relaxed, and settled down there. The Enemy knows that in fulfilling your God-given purpose on the earth, you will be a big hindrance to his agenda. So if he cannot stop you from starting, he will do everything he can to stop you from completing the journey.

Haran comes with a lot of offers. It promises you comfort and gives you a copy of what you are expecting in Canaan. "You were running the race nobly. Who has interfered in (hindered and stopped you from heeding and following the truth? (8) This evil persuasion is not from Him who called you [who invited you to freedom in Christ]" (Galatians 5:7-8,AMP).

Haran appeared to some people in the form of relationships. They settled down and forgot about the journey. For some, it was money. They came out of the systems of Babylon. They attended church but decided to pitch tents in Haran. Haran consumes time. Terah died there. What has made you so comfortable you don't desire an intimate walk with God? What is stopping you from fulfilling your destiny? It is standing as Haran.

Reject what the Devil presents and accept what God has for you. Don't allow appointments, positions, degrees, awards, and habits to become your destination, instead of the path to your destination.

God had to call Abraham out of Haran. "Now get thee out of thy country, and from thy kindred, and from thy father's house, unto a land that I will show thee" (Genesis 12:1, KJV).

A Christian on a journey of life in the absence of his maker is likened to a sheep without a shepherd. It is more of a spring without water. A river or a stream without water can't flow. A child without the spirit of the Father dwelling in him can't flow. You can't find a living creature in stagnant water by accident. Nothing good can be expected to come out of it.

Anyone whose life fits into the above automatically confines himself to the seat of a spectator in the congregation of the saints. While mates and equals are digging deep to achieve greatness with strength and spiritual input of God Most High, he stands afar off watching. Thus, he becomes a shadow of what he is supposed to be if he keeps moving away from divine direction. Many, if not all in this generation have a self-programmed, destructive agenda. They end up becoming errand boys and a mockery of a promising destiny. Solitary living results into shallow thoughts.

WALK IN FAITH

Abraham embarked on a journey from Haran to Canaan with his family, not sure which way to go. He had no map or GPS. He was not sure what to expect and was only armed with the word of God. "By faith Abraham, when he was called to go out into a place which he should after receive for an inheritance, obeyed; and he went out, not knowing wither he went" (Hebrews 11:8, KJV).

We must not imagine that because Ur of Chaldees was a city of idolatry, it was uncivilized and poor. Ur was a civilized place. If we view it from the eyes of mortals, we would say it was a great risk for Abraham to leave all that comfort to go to a strange land where he lived in tents.

Abraham would never have arrived in Canaan in the flesh. He had to have faith in God. For we can by no means walk with God except by faith.

"But without faith it is impossible to please him: for he that cometh to God must believe that he is, and that he is a rewarder of them that diligently seek him" (Hebrews 11:6, KJV).

"Faith is the substance of things hoped for, the evidence of things not seen. (2) For by faith the elders obtained a good report" (Hebrews 11:1-2, KJV).

Faith is holding God to His Word thereby committing Him to honor His promises. Faith is simply viewing circumstances from the standpoint of God, looking beyond what you see. You can be born again and still be carnal if you operate and lean on your five senses. You want to see, touch, hear, perceive, and taste before you believe.

> But Thomas, one of the twelve, called Didymus, was not with them when Jesus came. The other disciples therefore said unto him, we have seen the Lord. But he said unto them, Except I shall see in his hands the print of the nails, and put my finger into the print of the nails, and thrust my hand into his side, I will believe (John 20:24, KJV).

Jesus' response to Thomas was, "Blessed are they that have not seen me yet they believe" (John 20:28, KJV).

There are three kinds of men: the natural, carnal, and spiritual. The natural man is born into a human family and lives in his natural state without being a child of God. He does not have the Holy Spirit in him and lives his life driven by three human motivators: the lust of the flesh, lust of the eyes, and pride of life (1 John 2:15-17, KJV). He's unable to know, much less understand the deep things of God because he does not have the Spirit of God in him. Hence, he considers the things of the spirit as foolishness and rejects God and His Word.

The carnal man is born again into God's family but lives and behaves as a man in a natural state. He lives according to his carnal and fleshly desires. Instead of allowing the Holy Spirit to lead him, he depends on his senses. This produces ungodly works and the inability to grow in spiritual maturity and discernment. A carnal man often claims he is a Christian but demonstrates to the world that Christians are no different from anyone else (1 Peter 2:11-12, KJV).

The spiritual man is born again into God's family and lives in a spiritual state. He has the Holy Spirit and a new nature as he is not driven by the lust of the flesh, lust of the eyes, and pride. He can perceive spiritual things because he operates by the leading of the Holy Spirit.

You cannot go far with your senses because your eyes cannot see beyond their limits. It takes the eyes of the spirit to see beyond. Faith is simply accessing the wisdom of God and bringing it to the physical realm, which appears as foolishness to men. Just as the natural habitat of fish is water, the natural habitat of the believer is faith. The just shall live by faith (Hebrews 10:38, KJV).

Faith in God comes by knowing the truth, "So faith comes by hearing, and hearing by the word of God" (Romans 10:17, KJV). "Hearing" in this verse does not mean repetition but hearing, understanding, and obeying. Our relationship with God deepens the more our faith grows. Faith grows by meditating on the Word (Joshua 1:8, KJV). It grows by praying in the Holy Ghost (Jude 1:20, KJV). Hope says I will get it someday. Faith says I have it now. Hope says I will get strong. Faith says I am strong.

BUILDING TENTS

Abraham journeyed into a land flowing with milk and when he arrived everyone was building cities and erecting mighty structures. However, Abraham was building tents and looking for the city whose builder is God.

Prompted by faith he dwelt as a temporary resident

in the land which was designated in the promise of God, though he was like a stranger in a strange country, living in tents with Isaac and Jacob, fellow heirs with him of the same promise (10) For he was waiting expectantly and confidently looking forward to the city which has fixed and firm foundations whose architect and builder is God. (Hebrew 11:9-10 AMP)

Some people live as if the earth is the final destination. But Abraham knew there was much more than just a land flowing with milk and honey. He refused to be moved by the lifestyles of the people around him. He was not engrossed in mundane things. Paul, says in Philippians 3:7-8, KJV:

> But what things were given to me those I counted loss for Christ. (8) Yea doubtless and I count all things but loss for the excellency of the knowledge of Christ Jesus my Lord for I have suffered the loss of all things, and do count them but dung that I may win Christ.

Every achievement Paul ever attained, every title he ever had, he counted them loss for Christ. Building tents in this context does not mean you shouldn't build estates. It only points us to the direction where we do not place our confidence in earthly possessions. Every structure that was ever erected in times past is already old fashioned. Earthly treasures are temporary.

Lot became very wealthy. He had to be separated from Abraham and chose the place with the greener pasture. Abraham was not moved. In a matter of time, the city where Lot chose to reside was to be destroyed. Lot's wife had attached so much importance to the city, she found it hard to leave. "For where your treasure is, there will your heart be also" (Matthew 6:21, KJV). Her heart was in Sodom.

The angel had to pull them out of the city and warned them not to look back. Lot's wife's heart was in Sodom because he did not learn the principle of building tents. So she only ran a certain distance before she looked back to see how all her treasures were being destroyed. She became a pillar of salt.

Those who do not learn to build tents abandon the race because they lose a loved one; they lose property or their jobs. They quit the journey and blame God.

> Lay not up for yourselves treasures upon earth, where moth and rust doth corrupt, and where thieves break through and steal: (20) But lay up for yourselves treasures in heaven, where neither moth nor rust doth corrupt, and where thieves do not break through nor steal. (Matthew 6:19-20, KJV)

Jesus talked about the rich man who had great wealth. It was so much he had enough to feed him for years. He tied so much importance to his wealth that he failed to give the glory to God. That very night when he was boasting and celebrating, he died and left all the wealth he was bragging about (Luke 12:16-21, KJV).

"Money answers everything" is a fallacy that has made many Christians slaves to money, "A feast is made for laughter, and wine maketh merry: but money answereth all things" (Ecclesiastes 10:19, KJV). The Amplified Bible gives us a better interpretation of this passage, "Instead of repairing the breaches, the officials make a feast for laughter, serve wine to cheer life, and depend on tax money to answer for all of it" (Ecclesiastes 10:19, Amplified).

Money does not answer everything. As important as it is in our lives and the furtherance of the gospel, it is not the primary pursuit of the believer. "But seek ye first the kingdom of God and His righteousness; and all these things shall be added unto you" (Matthew 6:33, KJV).

We must learn like Paul to fix our eyes on the prize and not be distracted, "I press toward the mark for the prize of the high calling of God in Christ Jesus" (Philippians 3:14, KJV).

The Altar of Prayer

An altar is a system of authorization. It is a platform where the spirit realm interfaces with the physical realm. Abraham was a man of the altar. He came to understand that to journey far with God, he had to learn the way of the altar. Any man can work for God, but it takes a consistent prayer life to walk with Him. Many voices are on the earth, but it is only in the place of prayer that a man can master the voice of God. There are many spirits but only one Spirit of Truth. Abraham erected an altar specifically for the one and only true God.

It takes your prayer altar to be current with the dealings of God. "And he spake a parable unto them to this end, that men ought to pray and not faint" (Luke 18:1, KJV). When a man is not current with the dealings of God, frustration sets in. He begins to feel life is not moving at the pace he had expected. How current are you with God? I know you have a lot of things you want God to do, but what are the current dealings of God in your life?

Before you step out into the day, how well do you communicate with God? Do you settle your day in the place of prayer before you step out? You say you are always busy, but you will not be given an additional hour to the twenty-four hours you already have.

"And he withdrew himself into the wilderness to pray" (Luke 5:16, KJV). Jesus was never too busy to pray. He knew when to withdraw from every distraction. He showed us that prayer is very important. Sometimes you just have to shut down all your activities and spend quality time in the place of prayer.

The secret behind a man who lives a victorious life is his prayer altar. When David fought with Goliath, they both spoke on the strength of their prayer altars, "And the philistine said unto David, am I a dog, that thou comest to me with staves? And the philistine cursed David by his gods" (1 Samuel 17:43, KJV).

"Then said David to the Philistine, 'Thou comest to me with a sword, and with spear, and with shield: but I come to you in the name of the Lord of hosts, the God of the armies of Israel, whom thou hast defied'" (1 Samuel 17:4, KJV 5).

Before David embarked on any battle, he sought God's opinion. "And when David had enquired of the Lord, he said thou shall not go up, but fetch a compass behind them, and come upon them over against the mulberry trees" (2 Samuel 5:23, KJV).

David had access to several revelations from God of things to come because of the strength of his prayer altar. Saul prophesied, but he never really had a close relationship with

God. Saul was more concerned about the opinions of people. He wanted to be in everyone's good books. He knew God more as the God of Samuel. He never knew God was also merciful to the man who humbles himself and repents. Job had access to the secret of wealth on the strength of his prayer altar.

We don't need to erect physical altars today, for our hearts serve as altars.

CHAPTER FOUR

WHO IS GOD?

And Moses said to God, Behold, when I come to the Israelites and say to them, the God of your Father has sent me to you, and they say to me, what is His name? What shall I say to them? (14) And God said to Moses, I AM WHO I AM and WHAT I AM and I will BE WHAT I WILL BE, and He said, you shall say this to the Israelites : I AM has sent me to you. (Exodus 3:13, AMP)

Walking with God requires the knowledge of who He is.

The personality of God is embedded in His name. Whenever God appears, a dimension of Him is displayed. He can appear today as the God of mercy and visit again as the God of war. God is eternal in scope. You cannot define Him. You can only communicate an experience.

People worship different gods. They have the god of thunder, the god of the sea, the god of harvest, the god of fertility, and so forth. They worship every one of these gods.

When God spoke to Moses, He was letting him know how vast He is, and He cannot be restricted to a particular name, "I am what I am."

If you ask Noah who God is He will tell you He is the God of grace because in a world that was on the verge of annihilation, he found grace in the sight of God (Genesis 6:8, KJV). Abraham will tell you He is the covenant-keeping God, a friend, and the great provider. Jacob was not satisfied knowing God as the God of his father. He needed a personal encounter, and it was through that encounter that his name was changed from Jacob to Israel (Genesis 32:28, KJV).

Enoch walked with God. He was a man of the seventh generation and was able to peep into the future to receive a revelation of the second coming of Jesus. He was intimate enough with God to know He is the God of revelation. You cannot walk with God without knowing Him.

The world is being driven in a direction today that everyone needs to know God personally just like Daniel said, "Those that know their God they shall be strong and do exploit" (Daniel 11:32, KJV). You can read the entire Bible, graduate from the school of theology and still not know God. In fact, many who preach about God today are ignorant of who He is.

Every year, Hannah and her husband, like every other Christian, went to Shiloh. It was a religious practice to offer sacrifices unto the Lord of hosts. The time came when she was provoked and had no choice but to move past the priest, Eli. She had to talk to God by herself. It was in this place of prayer that she discovered what the priest never told her. The preacher may preach well, but there are things only God can tell you.

Hannah vocalized revelations of the holiness of God and His mighty power. These were not poems but revelations she got in the place of prayer. She decided to seek God by herself and not wait for the priest. She showed us a dimension of God the priest Eli did not show us. She made us know that God is never late.

Every name of God reveals a dimension of who He is. Moses will tell you the Lord is a man of war (Exodus 15:3, KJV). You should walk with Him well enough to know when He appears as the man of war. You should also know when He appears as the God of mercy. God seeks a personal relationship with each and every one of His children.

God wanted to draw the Israelites close to Himself, but they preferred Moses to be the mediator between them and Him. Some are afraid to come close to God because they know He will change many things in their lives.

The three Hebrew men in Babylon believed there is only one God, and the heat of the fire did not convince them otherwise. They refused to bow to any other god. The names of God you crammed are of no effect if you lack an experiential understanding of who He is.

Intimacy

> One thing have I desired of the Lord, that will I seek after; that I may dwell in the house of the Lord all the days of my life, to behold the beauty of the Lord, and to enquire in his temple. "When thou saidst, Seek ye my face; my heart said unto thee, Thy face, Lord, will I seek. (9) Hide not thy face far from me; put not thy servant away in anger. (Psalm 27:4, 8-9, KJV)

Walking with God becomes a religion when there is no hunger for intimacy. We are used to praying for blessings and miracles, but God wants us to have an intimate relationship with Him. The way you communicate with God is determined by your closeness to Him. One proof that you are physically healthy is your appetite for food. When people fall ill, they generally lose their appetite. The evidence of good spiritual health is your level of hunger for the things of God.

"Blessed are those who do hunger and thirst for righteousness for they shall be filled" (Matthew 5:6, KJV).

"In the last day of the feast, Jesus stood and cried, saying, if any man thirst, let him come unto me, and drink. (38) He that believeth on me, as the scripture hath said, out of his belly shall flow rivers of living water" (John 7:37-39, KJV).

After the religious feast, Jesus stood and addressed the crowd. He told them, "If any man thirst let him come." He said these words knowing that religion cannot quench spiritual thirst.

God told the people in Sinai to sanctify themselves and prepare for His coming. When He came, the Israelites stood at the foot of the mountain; they did not ascend. Moses, Aaron, Nadab, Abihu, and seventy of the elders of Israel went up the mountain. They saw the feet of God. They experienced a convincing manifestation of His presence. God did not harm them.

Moses did not stop there; he climbed up with Joshua, left him at a point, and climbed higher. This is an illustration of men interfacing with God at different levels. Some prefer to walk with God at a distance. The height to which a man ascends unto the hills of the Lord is determined by his hunger, dedication, and consecration. It is beyond appearing sanctimonious and pious, for the Psalmist asked, "Who shall ascend unto the hill of the Lord or who shall stand in Holy place? (4) He that hath a clean hand and a pure heart; who hath not lifted up his soul unto vanity, nor sworn deceitfully" (Psalm 24:3-4, KJV).

Moses walked with God to the extent he was never satisfied at one level. He had the hunger to know more about God. Moses stepped into eternity and became oblivious of time. However, the guys who were far away were counting the days. They were counting 40 days and becoming frustrated that Moses was taking too long. These are the kinds of people who come to church programs and because of their distance from God are always conscious of the time. They can hardly spend quality time in God's presence or in prayer.

Not too long, the Israelites sought an idol. The fact of the matter is, Aaron, who had reached a higher level and seen the feet of the Lord, built the idol for them. They all began to dance and worship this idol. They used the gold they brought from Egypt to build the calf. If you don't know why God is blessing you, you will soon begin to use your wealth to build idols.

Adam knew his wife and gave birth to children (Genesis 4:1-2). Moses knew God face-to-face and the result was immortality. His face shone with the glory of the Lord. People could not behold his face. In his old age, his eyes were not dim; he was climbing up the mountain. Adam was intimate with his wife and the result was children. Moses had an intimate relationship with God and even after he had died, the Devil was fighting over his body. It is not about the number of years you live. Your story can be like that of Methuselah. The only thing recorded of him is that he gave birth to sons and daughters.

Moses' hunger for God was insatiable. After all the encounters he had with Him, he still prayed, "Lord, show me thy glory" (Exodus 33:18). God said no man can see my face and live; any man that sees me will die. Only dead men come that close. Only men who are ready to lay their lives down on the altar of sacrifice can come that close.

Moses only saw the back of God, and he was able to trace Him back to the beginning. He saw the back of God and was able to write the book of Genesis. He was not there at creation, but he gave an account. When God gives you a pictorial revelation, just a flash, if you are to interpret that vision in the language of mortals, you can write an entire book.

Years after Moses had died, it was as if his prayer echoed into eternity. Who told you your prayers are wasted? The prayer did not die, when God the Son was on the mount of transfiguration, Moses and Elijah came there. Moses saw the glory of the Lord. Moses was a seeker, a man with a dangerous hunger. The things you pursue every day show what you are hungry for.

At age 120, God had to remind Moses he was about to cross the age limit humans are supposed to live. If He didn't remind him, he might have forgotten to die. God sent him up to Mount Nebo to die (Deuteronomy 32:49-50, KJV).

Are you just a Sunday Christian? How hungry are you for God? Are walking with Him daily? Are you satisfied like the guys at the foot of the mountain? Or do you want to ascend higher and higher into realms with God?

Jesus had twelve disciples and out of those twelve, three were very close to Him: Peter, James, and John. Out of those three, John was the closest. He was called the disciple whom Jesus loved. John was so close to Jesus people began to speculate he would not die until Jesus returns. He thought he knew Jesus enough until he was exiled to the island of Patmos and left there to die. "I was in the spirit on the Lord's day, and heard a voice behind me, a great voice as of trumpet" (Revelation 1:10). We don't know how long he had been on the island of Patmos, but it was the day he tuned into the spirit frequency that his stay began to make sense.

Every day is the Lord's Day. The day you decide to connect becomes your day. John encountered the Jesus he thought he knew, and he fell face flat like a dead man because only dead men come that close. After every revelation, he would hear a voice saying, "Come up hither."

God is too vast. You just can't get enough of Him. After every encounter, there is a need to go higher. Men who have touched something in God know the only life that is worth living is a life that is completely sold out to Him. How hungry are you for God? Your level of hunger will determine your walk with Him. It will show in your prayer life and desire for His Word.

IDOLS

An Idol is anything or anyone you love and place more value on than God. An idol could range from a character to an object.

> Thou shalt not make unto thee any graven image, or any likeness of anything that is in heaven above, or that is in the earth beneath, or that is in the water under the earth: (5) Thou shalt not bow down thyself to them, nor serve them: for I the Lord thy God am a jealous god, visiting the sin of the Fathers upon the children unto the third and fourth generation of them that hate me. (Exodus 20:4-6, KJV)

There are two types of jealousy:

1. A righteous and holy jealousy
2. An unrighteous and insecure jealousy

God's jealousy is righteous because He deserves our deepest affection and love.

An idol is anything or person you love, and value more than God. Idolatry starts in the heart. You crave, want, and enjoy being satisfied by what you treasure more than God. It is that thing that is loved more than God, that person you value more than God. "Who changed the truth of God into a lie, and worshipped and served the creature more than the creator, who is blessed forever" (Romans 1:25, KJV).

Today, many things have taken the attention of man from God. Your television can be an idol; that phone can be an idol. We are in a time people spend more time with their phones than they even do with their families. You can sit with your phone for hours. You can sit before the television without flinching all day long but ten minutes into prayer, you are already tired.

One of the biggest lies people tell themselves is that they are very busy. They don't have the time for anything that has to do with God.

"Master which is the greatest commandment in the law?" (Matthew 22:36, KJV).

> Jesus said unto him, Thou shalt love the Lord thy God with all thy soul, and with all thy mind. Any relationship that takes you away from God has become an idol. God does not deal with people by their outward appearance, but by the content of their heart. "These people honor me with their lips but their hearts are far away from me. (9) But in vain do they worship me, teaching for doctrines and the commandments of men" (Matthew 15:8-9, NIV).

"Son of man these men have set up their idols in their heart, and put stumbling block of their iniquity before their face; should I be enquired of at all by them?" (Ezekiel 14:3, KJV).

An idol can also be that character, habit, anger, pride, and lust. You derive pleasure from it and refuse to drop it on the altar of sacrifice. It will serve as nothing but a stumbling block.

> Two men went up into the temple enclosure to pray; the one a Pharisee, and the other a tax collector, (11) The Pharisee took his stand ostentatiously and began to pray thus before and with himself; God, I thank

you that I am not like the rest of men, extortions (robbers), swindlers [unrighteous in heart and life], adulterers or even like this tax collector here. (12) I fast twice a week; I give tithes of all that I gain. (13) But the tax collector, merely standing at a distance, would not even lift up his eyes to heaven, but kept striking his breast, saying, O God, be favorable (be gracious and merciful) to me, the especially wicked sinner that I am! (14) I tell you, this man went down to his home more justified (forgiven and made upright and in right standing with God), rather than the other man; for everyone who exalts himself will be humbled, by the who humbles himself will be exalted. (Luke 18:10-14, AMP)

The self-righteousness and pride of the Pharisee hindered him from accessing God. Every time he stood before God, that character became an idol in his life. He no longer saw it is not by his power or his might but by the grace of God. When you humble yourself, you look up to God for the supply of grace. You rely on Him alone. It shifts the focus from you to God.

A meeting was held in Sinai, and everyone was instructed to keep clean. They washed their clothes. The men were instructed not to go near their wives. They must appear clean because in that meeting, God would enter their midst.

Everyone came to that meeting outwardly clean. It happened that as the service began, Moses was gaining ascendance into the presence of God, he communed with God face to face. Meanwhile there where people down at the foot of the mountain, they never gained ascendance, just like people come to church and no matter how powerful the service, and the presence of the Lord comes down, they will still be on the ground level. While Moses had switched from the realm of time into eternity, and became oblivious of time, the people at the foot of the mountain were already wary of time, and they were counting days, and they made an idol and began to worship it. They were dancing and singing to this idol, while Moses was up communing with God. This a pointer to the fact people can come to church be singing and dancing, yet not unto God but unto an idol. Their lips are moving towards God but their hearts towards an idol. Christianity is beyond dressing sanctimonious and pious, whatever shifts your focus away from God has become an idol.

People give excuses for having idols. They tell you, "That's who I am." Rachel left her father's house but could not let go of her father's idol. She was not only married to Jacob but to His God now. Yet, she still held on to the idols. When Laban came looking for the idol, she hid it, sat on it, and gave an excuse to her father that she was in her period.

Now Rachel had taken the images, and put them in the camel's furniture, and sat upon them. And Laban searched all the tent, but found them not. (35) And she said to her father, let it not displease my Lord that I cannot rise u before thee; for the custom of women is upon me. And he searched but found not the images. (Genesis 31:34-35, KJV)

This is exactly what people do when the searchlight of the Holy Ghost exposes those secret idols. They prefer to make excuses than to surrender.

When last did you do a heart check like the psalmist? "Search me, O God, and know my heart: try me, and know my thoughts: (24) and see if there be any wicked way in me, ad lead me in the way everlasting" (Psalm 139:23-24, KJV). When the searchlight of the Holy Ghost comes, you will be surprised at the strange things that will be discovered.

CHAPTER FIVE
KINGDOM CITIZENS

"I will show thee, hear me, and that which I have seen I will declare (18) Which wise men have told from their fathers and have not hid it, (19) Unto whom alone the earth was given, and no stranger passed among them" (Job 15:17-19, KJV).

Our attention is drawn to the words of Eliphaz the Temanite, one of Job's friends. He spoke concerning a people who were able to pass wisdom and order from generation to generation. It's just like a community with a cultural belief, certain laws, and a pattern that was passed on from one generation to another. When strangers enter a community, they often come with a different language, culture, belief system, and religion. After some time, they either influence the community with their culture or they are influenced.

The colonial masters did this to the countries they colonized. They influenced them and taught them their language, lifestyles, cultures, and traditions. Years after those countries gained independence, you can still see the impact of the colonial masters on them. Some even abandoned most of their cultural practices and adopted foreign names and lifestyles. This means many of the age-long practices of this people were erased as time progressed. However, some places have maintained their cultural practices regardless of the influence of the colonial masters. They have successfully passed on those beliefs and rituals from one generation to another.

Eliphaz, communicating within this context, said this wisdom was passed from generation to generation. The truth was not corrupted because they did not give room for aliens to do so.

Every believer is a representative of the kingdom of God. The kingdom has a language. The kingdom has a culture and belief system. The very fact that we are in the world does not mean we are of the world. "If you belong to the world, the world would treat you with affection and would love you as its own. But because you are not of the world [no longer one with it], but I have chosen (selected) you out of the world, the world hates (detest) you" (John 15:19, AMP). By coming into Christ, we have come into another government that is not regulated by mortal men.

The essence of our subscription to this system is not just to bear the name Christian but that our characters would be the plumbline to convict others of their sinful ways. The Holy Spirit guides us to a full understanding of this heavenly government: "Howbeit when He, the Spirit of truth, is come, he will guide you into all truth: for he shall not speak of Himself; but whatsoever he shall hear, that shall he speak: and he will shew you things to come" (John 16:13, KJV). This helps us understand we cannot do anything as kingdom citizens on the earth without the Holy Spirit, the Spirit of Truth; only He can guide us into all truth. Any other spirit you submit to will only guide you into lies.

We are ambassadors of the kingdom.

"For which I am an ambassador in bonds, that therein I may speak boldly, as I ought to speak" (Ephesians 6:20, KJV).

"Now then we are ambassadors for Christ, as though God did beseech you by us: we pray you in Christ's stead, be reconciled to God" (2 Corinthians 5:20, KJV).

An ambassador does not belong to the country to which he is sent. A believer is not a citizen of this world but of heaven. "Jesus answered, my kingdom is not of this world: if my kingdom were of this world, then would my servants fight, that I should not be delivered to the Jews: but now is my kingdom not from hence" (John 18:36).

An ambassador enters a country not to fulfill his personal interests or chase his personal dreams and ambitions but to represent the interests of his country. "Whereupon O King Agrippa, I was not disobedient to the heavenly vision" (Acts 26:19, KJV). We don't operate as kingdom citizens by explanations but by instructions. People want explanations for everything before they walk with God. An ambassador is given instructions by which he operates. You are not called to be creative but to yield to instructions.

Mode of Communication

> For the Lord spoke thus to me with His strong hand [upon me] and warned and instructed me not to walk in the way of this people, saying (12) Do not call a conspiracy (or hard or holy] all that this people will call conspiracy [or hard or holy]; neither be in fear of what they fear, nor [make others afraid and] in dread. (Isaiah 8:11-12, KJV)

As kingdom citizens, we have a mode of communication. We communicate the Word of God that abides in us. It must be demonstrated in our conversions. The above scripture says we should not walk in the way of the world by saying what they say. When we say what they want us to, we begin to believe what they believe and become afraid of what they are afraid of.

"When men are cast down then thou shalt say there is a lifting up; and he shall save the humble person" (Job 22:29, KJV). When the world says there is a casting down, the citizens of the kingdom say there is a lifting. We don't speak according to the trends of this world but what is written in the Word of God. "And he said, I heard thy voice in the garden, and I was afraid, because I was naked, and I hid myself" (Genesis 3:10, KJV).

Fear is not a spirit of the kingdom. Where did you learn that? Adam had subscribed to another culture whose language he was communicating. That's how fear entered.

"Thy word is a lamp unto my feet and a light unto my path" (Psalm 119:105, KJV).

"O how I love thy law. It is my meditation all day. 98) Thou through thy commandment hast made me wiser than mine enemies: for they are ever with me. (99) I have more understanding than all my teachers: for thy testimonies are my meditation" (Psalm 119:97-99, KJV).

"Through thy precepts I get understanding: therefore I hate every false way" (Psalm 119:104, KJV).

David revealed to us that the secret behind his wisdom was the Word of God. He meditated on it every day and became wiser than the ancients. He demonstrated how he hated evil and walking the false way because he had gained understanding from the Word of God. You cannot walk with God without loving Him, and you cannot love God without loving and obeying His Word.

If the words that come out of your mouth are contrary to the Word of God, you cannot walk with Him. "Can two walk together, except they be agreed?" (Amos 3:3, KJV).

> But the tongue can no man tame, for it is an unruly evil, full of deadly poison. (9) Therewith bless we God, even the Father; and therewith curse we men, which are made after the similitude of God. (10) Out of the same mouth proceedeth blessing and cursing. My brethren, these things ought not to so to be. (11) Doth a fountain send forth at the same place sweet water and bitter, (12) can the fig tree, my brethren, bear olive berries? Either a vine, figs? So can no fountain both yield salt and fresh water and fresh. (13) Who is a wise man and endued with knowledge among you? Let him show out of a good conversation his works with the meekness of wisdom. (James 3:8-13, KJV)

Not every word of wisdom is from God. There is earthly, sensual wisdom (James 3:15, KJV). You cannot curse with the same mouth you use to bless. It is not the way of the kingdom you represent. If you want to know who a man is, wait until he talks. If people cannot identify you based on your conversations as a Christian, something is wrong. A true believer cannot talk without making reference to the Word of God; it is a key reference point.

Some people will say forget about the Bible; let's face reality, but no reality exists outside the Word of God. The Bible might be old, but the Word is ever fresh; it is ever new. It touches every aspect of life. Times will change; seasons will change; kings will reign and be replaced; technology will advance, but the Word of God remains forever.

LOVE

Love is a fruit of the Spirit (Galatians 5:22, KJV). As a kingdom citizen, one of the fruits the world will see in your life is love. You cannot claim to love God if you hate your neighbor. "If a man say, I love God and hateth his brother, he is a liar; for he that loveth not his brother whom he hath seen, how can he love God whom he hath not seen" (1 John 4:20, KJV).

Paul, speaking in the book of 1 Corinthians 13:2-3, AMP says:

> And if I have prophetic powers (the gift of interpreting the divine will and purpose), and understanding all

secret truths and mysteries and possess all knowledge, and is I have sufficient faith so that I can remove mountains, but have not love (God's love in me) I am nothing (a useless nobody). (3) Even if I dole out all that I have to the poor in providing food, and if I surrender my body to be burned or in order that I may glory, but have not love (God's love in me), I gain nothing.

Regardless of what you do in life, the position you attain, the accolades you receive, if you do not have love, it's all a waste. God is love and love is God. You cannot claim to be a child of God if you don't demonstrate love.

Love is a commitment to meet the needs of another without expecting anything in return. The closer you get to God, the more He fills your heart with love, and it begins to reflect on your relationship with people. People's attitudes to others are usually a reflection of how they see themselves. If you see yourself as one created in the image of God, you will view others in the same way.

"And the second is like unto it, thou shalt love thy neighbor as thyself" (Matthew 22:39, AMP). Jesus illustrated to us who our neighbors are with a parable (The Good Samaritan) about a man who was attacked on his way to Jericho. The priest and

Levite passed by and ignored him, but a Samaritan came, rescued the man and paid for his medical bills. Jesus pointed out to us that this Samaritan was a true neighbor. The love demonstrated here shows love is not partial. The Samaritan, regardless of his background, came to the aid of the man. Love does not discriminate. The Samaritan was on a journey. He could have gone his way like the priest and the Levite, but he had compassion on the man. Love is compassionate. The Samaritan did not only feel sorry for the man, he responded by meeting his needs.

True love anticipates the needs of others. It seeks to meet the needs of others without them asking. Love is sacrificial. Do you still give to get a reward? Do you give to receive applause and gain popularity? The Samaritan did not know this wounded man from anywhere. Yet, he paid the bills and told the innkeeper if there were additional costs, he should add it to his bill, which he would pay when he returned. The Samaritan did this good deed without calling attention to himself. Some people cannot give without announcing it to the world.

Love is patient. We see it displayed in the actions of the Samaritan. He took his time to give the man first aid treatment and bandaged his wounds.

Love is not selfish. He sacrificed his donkey to carry the man. Some people will never sacrifice their time to work for God.

Love is not self-centered. God so loves the world that He gave. He had no conditions attached. He loved us so much He gave His beloved Son. There is no love without giving.

You show your love for God by how you treat the people around you. In today's world, people believe you should only love those who love you, care for those who care for you, and give to those who give to you. If you adopt this lifestyle, what will differentiate you from the world? Jesus said love your enemies, not only those who love you.

> But I say unto you love your enemies, bless them curse you, do good to them that hate you and pray for them which despitefully use you and persecute you, (45) That ye may be the children of your Father which is in heaven: for he maketh his sun to rise on the evil and on the good, and sendeth rain on the just and on the unjust. (Matthew 5:44-45, AMP)

If you must be begged to forgive before you forgive, you haven't encountered the spirit of love. An encounter with the spirit of love causes you to forgive people in advance. Love is not emotions. Love is a spirit "For God hath not given us the spirit of fear; but of power, and of love and of sound mind"

(2Timothy 1:7, KJV). Jesus taught what He practiced. He demonstrated everything He taught us. "The former treatise have I made, O Theophilus, of all that Jesus both began to do and teach" (Acts 1:1, KJV). Today, we have more love preachers than love practitioners. Some people will paste the sticker of love on their doorposts, but when you get into the house, the atmosphere is full of hatred.

Jesus hung on the cross in such pain and agony. He was denied water and beaten beyond recognition by the people He came to save. He was thirsty; they gave Him vinegar. Yet, right there in that condition He prayed: "Father forgive them, for they know not what they are doing." Jesus demonstrated to us that you cannot separate love and forgiveness. Regardless of what anybody does to you, you must forgive, "If ye forgive men their trespasses, your heavenly father will also forgive you, (15) But if ye forgive not men their trespasses, neither will your father forgive your trespasses" (Matthew 6:14, KJV). If God should respond to you according to your actions, you won't be redeemed. If God forgives you the way you forgive others, will you make it to heaven?

Holiness

Holiness means to be in a class of your own, distinct from anything that has ever existed or will ever exist. Holy means sacred or set apart from something unto something or someone else. "There is none holy as the Lord, for there is none beside thee: neither is there any rock like our God" (1 Samuel 2:2, KJV). "But as he which hath called you s holy, so be ye holy in all manner of conversation" (1 Peter1:15, KJV). Holiness can be defined as living a godly lifestyle or God-kind of life. Holiness is living a standard of life that is pleasing to God. "When a man's ways please the Lord, he maketh even his enemies to be at peace with him" (Proverbs 16:7, KJV). Holiness is not just a way of life but God's standard of living.

To be holy is to live a life that is pleasing to God when nobody sees you. It is what you do in the secret, keeping away from evil when no man sees you. "Thou blind Pharisee, cleanse first that which is within the cup and platter, that the outside of them may be clean also" (Matthew 23:26, KJV).

That it is trending does not mean it is right. The standard by which Christians operate is not the same as the world. God wants to look down from heaven and see a people who are separated unto Him.

Enoch separated himself unto God. In the days of Noah when

sin and evil were the trends, Noah separated himself unto God. Can God boast of you like He boasted about Job? "And the Lord said unto Satan, 'Hast thou considered my servant Job, that there is none like him in the earth, a perfect and an upright man, one that feareth God and escheweth evil?'" (Job 1:8). Job was a perfect man, not because he did not make mistakes but because he feared God and hated evil. You must hate iniquity to live a holy life.

You must desire holiness above anything and pursue it. You must not be ignorant of the devices of the Devil in these last days. Today, you can browse the internet and find many images, videos, articles, and such like that have dragged the hearts of many away from God. You turn on the television and find programs that promote stealing, fornication, adultery, as well as drug and alcohol abuse. We must be wise enough not to give in to the crafts of the Devil. We must call what is evil, evil and not try to cover it up. "Woe unto them that call evil good and good evil; that put darkness for light and light for darkness; that put bitter for sweet and sweet for bitter" (Isaiah 5:20, KJV).

To be holy, one must be connected to God as the source. You are holy because you have been bought by the blood of Jesus.

"What! Know ye not that your body is the temple of the Holy Ghost which is in you, which ye have of God, and ye are not your own? (20) For ye are bought with a price: therefore glorify God in your body, and in your spirit, which are God's" (1 Corinthians 6:19-20, KJV).

"He has saved us to live a holy life not because of anything we have done but because of His own purpose and grace" (2 Timothy 1:9, NIV).

Our manner of life must reflect holiness because God is holy.

To the world, living a holy life is foolishness. However, the Bible says the fear of God is the beginning of wisdom. "The fear of the Lord is the beginning of wisdom: and the knowledge of the holy is understanding" (Proverbs 9:10). The fear of God is not to dread God and run away but to hate evil, "The fear of the Lord is to hate evil: pride, and arrogance, and the evil way, and the forward mouth, do I hate" (Proverbs 8:13, KJV).

Seek the Lord in prayer and study His Word. Avoid every appearance of evil (1 Thessalonians 5:22, KJV). Today, we find more Christians on Sunday than on the remaining days of the week. Our lights are meant to shine before men every day. God would not ask us to be holy without giving us the help we need to make us that way. That is why we have received the Holy Spirit in us to work on us from the inside out. "Be confident of this very thing that he which hath begun a good work in you will perform it until the day of Jesus Christ" (Philippians 1:6, KJV). This indicates that the pursuit of holiness cannot be achieved without the indwelling of the Holy Spirit. He shines light on every area that needs to be dealt with. He searches the contents of your heart and deals with every stumbling block to righteous living.

Better Is the End

"Better is the end of a thing than the beginning thereof" (Ecclesiastes 7:8, KJV). Solomon, the preacher, the son of David, was famously known for his depth of wisdom. He said the end of a thing is better than the beginning. In other words, for everything we do and each journey we embark, we must envisage the end.

> For which of you, intending to build a tower sitteth not down first, and counteth the cost, whether he have sufficient to finish it. (29) Lest haply, after he hath laid the foundation, and is not able to finish it, all that behold it begin to mock him. (30) Saying, this man began to build and was not able to finish… (33) So likewise, whosoever he be of you that forsaketh not all that he hath, he cannot be my disciple. (Luke 14:28-30, 33 KJV)

God is not only concerned with you starting the race; he is very much concerned with you finishing as well. Many have started well. They were burning for God but after sometime, they derailed; they shifted ground.

The Devil does not have a problem with you starting, and sometimes he waits patiently before he attacks. That's why after many years you find a lot of people who were die-hard followers of God backslide. The Devil waited a while and then he pounced on them.

In other instances, many took off like jets and crashed along the way. This race is long distance; it is not a sprint. Don't take off like the Prodigal Son. He walked up to his father and requested, "Father give me the portion of goods that falleth to me" (Luke 15:12, KJV). His first prayer was centered on "give me." There are many in the church today who focus on "give me." Some are not patient enough. That is why they quickly look for alternatives.

The Prodigal Son did not calculate the cost. He just decided to embark on the journey without considering the end. When the harsh realities of life began to hit, he was soon broke. However, he came to his senses and this time around he said, "I will go back to my father acknowledging the fact that I have sinned against heaven, and before him and I will ask him to make me as one of his hired servants" (Luke 15:18-19, KJV). This time around, he said "make me." Allow God to make you, break you, and mold you. God takes you through a process because He will not build with a stone that he has not tried.

> Consider it wholly joyful, my brethren, whenever you are enveloped in or encounter trials of any sort or fall into various temptations. (3) Be assured and understand that the trial and proving of your faith bring out endurance and steadfastness and patience. (4) But let endurance and steadfastness and patience have full play and do a thorough work, so that you may be [people] perfectly and fully developed [with no defects], lacking nothing. (James 1:2-4, AMP)

You have heard of Billy Graham, but what about Chuck Templeton or Bron Clifford? Have you ever heard of them? Billy Graham wasn't the only preacher packing auditoriums in 1945. Chuck Templeton and Bron Clifford were accomplishing the same thing and more. All three young men were in their mid-twenties. One seminary president after hearing Chuck Templeton preach one evening to an audience of thousands called him "the most gifted and talented young man in America."

Templeton and Graham were friends. Both were extraordinary

preachers. In those early years, most observers would probably have put their money on Templeton.

Bron Clifford was yet another gifted, twenty-five-year-old fireball. In 1945, many believed Clifford was the most gifted and powerful preacher the church had seen in centuries. At the age of twenty-five, young Clifford touched more lives, influenced more leaders, and set more attendance records than any other clergyman his age in American history. National leaders vied for his attention. He was tall, handsome, intelligent, and eloquent.

In 1945, all three came shooting out of the starting blocks like rockets. Just five years later, Templeton left the ministry to pursue a career as a radio and television commentator and newspaper columnist. Templeton had decided he was no longer a believer in Christ.

What about Clifford? By 1945, Clifford had lost his family, his ministry, his health, and then his life. Alcohol and financial irresponsibility had done him in. He wound up leaving his wife and their two children. His last job was selling cars in Texas. He died as John Haggai put it, "unwept and unsung." In 1945, three young men with extraordinary gifts were preaching the gospel to thousands across the nation and within ten years only one of them was still on track for Jesus.

Therefore whosoever heareth these sayings of mine, and doeth them, I will liken him unto a wise man, which built his house upon a rock: (25) And the rain descended, and the floods came, and the winds blew, and beat upon the house; and it fell not: for it was founded upon a rock. (26) And every one that heareth these sayings of mine, and doeth them not, shall be likened unto a foolish man, which built his house upon sand: 27) And the rain descended, and the floods came, and the winds blew, and beat upon that house; and it fell: and great was the fall of it. (Matthew 7:24-27, KJV)

To build a house on a rock takes time. It takes sacrifice and extra effort unlike building on sand. This was an illustration of two people who did not only hear the Word of God, but they obeyed it. They followed the word daily.

The people who had taken root in the Word of God, who patiently stood on the Word of God, did not forget God when the rain of blessings came from above. When the storms of life came, they stood their ground.

Mighty men have fallen. Many Christians today are still falling by the wayside. Some have become very comfortable and forget about God. Others could not withstand the storms of life and forsook God. To make it to the end, you must rely on God's supply of grace. It is not by power or might. There is a place of personal discipline.

> Now every athlete who goes into training conducts himself temperately and restricts himself in all things. They do it to win a wreath that will soon wither, but we do it to receive a crown of eternal blessedness that cannot wither (26) Therefore I do not run uncertainly without definite aim. I do not box like one beating the air and striking without adversary. (27) But (like a boxer) I buffet my body [handle it roughly, discipline it by hardships] and subdue it, for fear that after proclaiming to others the Gospel and things pertaining to it, I myself should become unfit [not stand the test, be unapproved and rejected as a counterfeit]. (1 Corinthians 9:25-27, AMP)

Set your eyes on the prize. Press for the crown. Do not be moved by distractions. Forget the achievements of yesterday and keep pressing for that crown. Better is the end of a thing; therefore, you must envisage this end, which is the crown. If not, you will receive a counterfeit crown here on the earth and forget all about God.

The words of Paul should be written on the walls of the hearts of everyone on this journey, "I have fought the good (worthy, honorable, and noble) fight. I have kept (firmly held) the faith" (2 Timothy 4:7, KJV).

You must fight because no man who puts his hand to the plough and looks back is fit for the kingdom (Luke 9:62, KJV).

REFERENCE

1. *Sit, Stand, and Walk* by Watchman Nee

2. *Chemistry of the Blood* by pastor M.R. Dehaan, M.D

3. *Back to the Cross* by Watchman Nee

4. *Finishing Strong* by Steve Farrar

www.ingramcontent.com/pod-product-compliance
Lightning Source LLC
Chambersburg PA
CBHW070937160426
43193CB00011B/1715